CUPCAKE COOKBOOK

Amazing Cupcake Recipes in Your Own Cupcake Cookbook!

(Life Is Better When You Have a Sweet Bite)

Kimberley Carbone

Published by Sharon Lohan

© **Kimberley Carbone**

All Rights Reserved

Cupcake Cookbook: Amazing Cupcake Recipes in Your Own Cupcake Cookbook! (Life Is Better When You Have a Sweet Bite)

ISBN 978-1-7776245-4-5

All rights reserved. No part of this guide may be reproduced in any form without permission in writing from the publisher except in the case of brief quotations embodied in critical articles or reviews.

Legal & Disclaimer

The information contained in this book is not designed to replace or take the place of any form of medicine or professional medical advice. The information in this book has been provided for educational and entertainment purposes only.

The information contained in this book has been compiled from sources deemed reliable, and it is accurate to the best of the Author's knowledge; however, the Author cannot guarantee its accuracy and validity and cannot be held liable for any errors or omissions. Changes are periodically made to this book. You must consult your doctor or get professional medical advice before using any of the suggested remedies, techniques, or information in this book.

Table of contents

Part 1 1
Introduction 2
1. Classic Vanilla Cupcakes 3
2. Red Velvet Cupcakes 4
3. Chocolate Cupcakes 6
4. Boston Cream Cupcakes 8
5. Brown Butter Cupcakes 10
6. Rose Cupcakes 11
7. Mocha Cupcakes 13
8. Chocolate Chips Cupcakes 14
9. Gingerbread Cupcakes 16
10. Coconut Cupcakes 17
11. Blackberry Cupcakes 19
12. Lime Cupcakes 21
13. Orange Cupcakes 24
14. Carrot Cupcakes 25
15. Chocolate Cherry Cupcakes 27
16. Raspberry Cupcakes 28
17. Grapefruit Poppy Seeds Cupcakes 30
18. Lemon And Poppy Seeds Cupcakes 32
19. Apple Cupcakes 34
20. Peach Cupcakes 35
21. Triple Berry Cupcakes 37
22. Tropical Mango Cupcakes 38

23. Banana And Nut Cupcakes With Ricotta And Honey Frosting 40
24. Strawberry Cupcakes 41
25. Blueberry And Oatmeal Cupcakes 43
26. Pear And Chocolate Cupcakes 44
27. All Maple Cupcakes 46
28. Peanut Butter Cupcakes 48
29. Liquor Buttercream Cupcakes 49
30. Chocolate And Peanut Butter Cupcakes 51
Conclusion 53
Part 2 54
Introduction 55
Learn About Sweetness In Life 55
Chapter 1: Delicious Fruity Cupcakes 58
Recipe 01: Raspberries Cupcakes 58
Recipe 02: Orange Flavored Cupcakes 59
Recipe 03: Vanilla Bean Cupcakes 60
Recipe 04: Strawberry Jam Cupcakes 61
Recipe 05: Buttermilk Cupcakes 62
Chapter 2: Delicious Flavors Of Cupcakes 63
Recipe 06: Chocolate Cupcakes 63
Recipe 07: Jelly Bean Cupcakes 64
Recipe 08: Maltesers Cupcakes 65
Recipe 09: Coffee Flavored Cupcakes 66
Recipe 10: Pink Coconut Cupcakes 67
Recipe 11: Cocoa Cupcakes 68
Recipe 12: Dark Chocolate Cupcakes 69

Recipe 13: Pumpkin Cupcakes 70
Chapter 3: Soft And Sweet Cupcakes 72
Recipe 14: Caramel Cupcakes 72
Recipe 15: Almond Meal Cupcakes 73
Recipe 16: Lemon Zest Cupcake 74
Recipe 17: Sour Cream Mix Cupcake 74
Recipe 18: Lime And Coconut Cupcake 75
Recipe 19: Cream Cheese Devil Cupcakes 76
Chapter 4: Easy To Make Cupcakes 79
Recipe 20: Coconut With Dark Chocolate Cupcakes 79
Recipe 21: Licorice Cupcakes 80
Recipe 22: White Chocolate Cupcakes 81
Recipe 23: Mango Puree Cupcakes 82
Recipe 24: Raspberries White Choco Cupcakes 83
Recipe 25: Red Cupcakes 84
Cupcakes Recipes 86
Chocolate Cupcakes With Caramel Frosting 86
Chocolate Beer Cupcakes With Whiskey Filling And Irish Cream Icing 88
Dark Chocolate Bacon Cupcakes 90
Chili Chocolate Cupcakes With Chili Cream Cheese Frosting 91
Cherry Coke Cupcakes 93
German Chocolate Cupcakes 94
Chocolate Chip Cheesecake Cupcakes 96
Chocolate-Orange Cupcakes With Pistachio Buttercream 98
Lemon Cupcakes 100
Lemon Frosted Carrot Cake Cupcakes 101

Real Strawberry Cupcakes 103
Sin-Fully Delicious Chocolate Cupcakes 105
Frosted Peppermint Mini Bites 107
Conclusion 109

Part 1

Introduction

You can make a rock party with simple ingredients and minimal effort. I know you're wondering how. The answer is simple. Bake cupcakes. From standards like vanilla or chocolate cupcake to intense flavor combinations like peanut butter and chocolate, liquor or mocha, this book got you covered in every situation.

1. Classic Vanilla Cupcakes

Nothing can beat a homemade vanilla cupcake, it so simple, yet so good, plus your house will smell heavenly. It can't get any better.

Makes: 12 cupcakes
Time: 50 min
Ingredients
Cupcakes

2 cups all-purpose flour
- 1 cup yogurt
- ¾ cup butter
- 2 tsp baking powder
- 2 tsp vanilla extract
- 1 cup sugar
- ½ tsp salt
- 2 eggs

Frosting

1/2 cup butter
- 2 cups powdered sugar
- 1 tbsp. cream
- 1 tsp vanilla extract

Directions
Preheat oven at 350 F. Line a cupcake tin with cupcake liners and set aside. In a big bowl cream butter and sugar together, using a hand mixer.
Add the eggs and vanilla extract and beat well. Then add the yogurt and beat again. In another bowl mix all-purpose flour, salt and baking powder. Pour the dry Ingredients to the wet Ingredients and mix just until incorporating.
Divide the batter in the cupcake tin and Bake in your preheated oven for 22-25 minutes. Let the Cupcakes cool completely before frosting. While the Cupcakes are cooling prepare the frosting. In a big stand mixer mix together butter, powdered sugar, cream and vanilla extract until creamy and very smooth, it may take 3-5 minutes. Pour the frosting in a piping bag and frost the Cupcakes. Enjoy.

2. Red Velvet Cupcakes

These beautifully red Cupcakes are topped with a delicious cream cheese frosting, and have a light hint of chocolate coming from cocoa powder.
Makes: 12 Cupcakes
Time: 45 min

Ingredients
Cupcakes

1 ¼ all-purpose flour
- 2 tbsp. cocoa powder
- 2 tsp red food coloring
- ½ tsp salt
- 1 tsp baking soda
- ½ cup canola oil
- ½ cup sugar
- ½ cup buttermilk
- 2 eggs
- 1 ½ tsp white vinegar
- 1 tsp vanilla extract

Cream cheese frosting

½ stick butter
- 6 ounces cream cheese
- 1 cup powdered sugar
- 1 tsp vanilla extract

Directions

Preheat oven at 375 degrees. Line a cupcake tin with cupcake liners and set aside.
In a big bow whisk oil, eggs, vanilla extract and sugar until well incorporated.
Add buttermilk and mix again.
In another bowl mix flour, red color powder, cocoa powder and salt.
Pour the dry Ingredients to the wet Ingredients and then mix well.
Mix baking soda with vinegar and pour it in the batter, mixing well and fast.
Divide the batter in the cupcake forms and bake in your preheated oven for 20-25 minutes.

Let the Cupcakes cool completely before frosting them. To prepare the frosting beat butter, sugar and cream cheese very well using a hand or a stand mixer. Pour the frosting in a pastry bag and pipe it over Cupcakes. Enjoy.

3. Chocolate Cupcakes

These double chocolate Cupcakes are a little piece of heaven. The cake is full of chocolate flavor and the frosting is a simple chocolate ganache, which makes them even more chocolaty.

Makes: 12 Cupcakes
Time: 45 min
Ingredients
Cupcakes

1 ½ cups all-purpose flour
- ¾ cup cocoa powder
- 2 tsp baking powder
- ½ tsp salt
- 1 ¼ cups sugar
- 2 eggs
- ½ cup oil
- ½ cup buttermilk
- ½ cup hot coffee

Ganache frosting
- 1 cup dark chocolate chips
- 1/2 cup cream

Directions

Preheat oven at 375 degrees. Line a cupcake tin with cupcake liners and set aside. In a big bow beat eggs and sugar until light and fluffy. Whisk oil and sugar until well incorporated. Add buttermilk and hot coffee and mix again. In another bowl mix flour, cocoa powder, baking powder, and salt.

Pour the dry Ingredients to the wet Ingredients and then mix well.

Divide the batter in the cupcake forms and Bake in your preheated oven for 22-25 minutes. Let the Cupcakes cool completely before frosting them. To prepare the frosting heat the cream in a small sauce pan. Remove from heat and add the chocolate chips. Whisk them well until completely melted. Let the ganache cool almost completely, and then frost Cupcakes using a small butter knife or spoon. Enjoy.

4. Boston Cream Cupcakes

Imagine all the flavors and textures or a Boston cream cake, packed in cupcake form. It is one my favorite Cupcakes ever.

Makes: 12 Cupcakes
Time: 55 min
Ingredients
Cupcakes

1 ½ cups all-purpose flour
- 2 tsp baking powder
- ½ tsp salt
- 1 cup sugar
- 2 eggs
- 3/4 cup butter
- ½ cup buttermilk
- 1 tsp vanilla extract

Pastry cream

1 ½ cups cream
- 2 egg yolks
- 1/3 cup sugar
- 1 tbsp. corn starch
- Ganache frosting

- 1 cup dark chocolate chips
- 1/2 cup cream

Directions

Start by preparing the pastry cream. Whisk well all Ingredients together and cook over low heat until the cream gets thick and shiny. You should stir the mixture during cooking, so it cooks uniformly and doesn't stick to the pan.

Once it is cooked remove from the heat, cover with cling film and let cool in the fridge.

Preheat oven at 375 degrees. Line a cupcake tin with cupcake liners and set aside.

In a big bow cream butter and sugar until light and fluffy. Beat in the eggs one by one and then add buttermilk and vanilla extract.

In another bowl mix flour, baking powder, and salt. Pour the dry Ingredients to the wet Ingredients and then mix well.

Divide the batter in the cupcake forms and Bake in your preheated oven for 22-25 minutes.

Let the Cupcakes cool completely before filling and frosting them.

To prepare the frosting heat the cream in a small sauce pan. Remove from heat and add the chocolate chips. Whisk them well until completely melted.

Let the ganache cool completely before covering the Cupcakes. With a sharp knife open a small hole on each cupcake and add 1 tbsp. pastry cream, and then frost Cupcakes using a small butter knife or spoon.

Enjoy.

5. Brown Butter Cupcakes

Imagine a dense cake, covered with a dense buttercream and chocolate frosting. Sounds amazing and is so easy to make.
Makes: 12 Cupcakes
Time: 45 min
Ingredients
Cupcakes

2 ¼ cups cake flour
- 2 tsp baking powder
- ½ tsp salt
- 1 cup sugar
- 3 eggs
- 1 cup butter
- 3/4 cup milk
- 1 tsp vanilla extract

Chocolate buttercream

1/2 cup dark chocolate chips
- 1/2 cup butter
- 2 cups powdered sugar
- 2 tbsp. cocoa
- 4 tbsp. whipping cream

Directions

Preheat oven at 375 degrees. Line a cupcake tin with cupcake liners and set aside. Melt butter and let it slightly brown, being careful not to burn it.

In a big bowl beat butter and sugar until well mixed. Beat in the eggs one by one and then add milk and vanilla extract.

In another bowl mix flour, baking powder, and salt. Pour the dry Ingredients to the wet Ingredients and then mix well.

Divide the batter in the cupcake forms and Bake in your preheated oven for 22-25 minutes. Let the Cupcakes cool completely before frosting them. To prepare the frosting melt chocolate in a double boiler or microwave.

In a big bowl beat butter, sugar, cocoa and cream together until light and fluffy. Add the melted chocolate and beat until well incorporated.

Frost the Cupcakes with a butter knife or a small spoon Enjoy.

6. Rose Cupcakes

These delicious Cupcakes have a very nice touch of rose flavor which matched perfectly with the white chocolate buttercream.

Makes: 12 Cupcakes
Time: 45 min
Ingredients
Cupcakes

1 1/2 cups cake flour
- 1 ½ tsp baking powder
- ½ tsp salt
- 3/4 cup sugar
- 1 tsp of vanilla extract
- 2 eggs
- 1/2 cup oil
- 1/2 cup Greek yogurt
- 1 tsp rose water

White Chocolate buttercream

1/4 cup of dark chocolate chips
- 1/2 cup butter
- 2 cups powdered sugar
- 2 tbsp. whipping cream

Directions

Preheat oven at 375 degrees. Line a cupcake tin with cupcake liners and set aside. In a big beat eggs and sugar. Beat in oil and then add yogurt, rose water and vanilla extract. In another bowl mix flour, baking powder, and salt. Pour the dry Ingredients to the wet Ingredients and then mix well.
Divide the batter in the cupcake forms and Bake in your preheated oven for 22-25 minutes. Let the Cupcakes cool completely before frosting them.

To prepare the frosting melt chocolate in a double boiler or microwave.

In a big bowl beat butter, sugar and cream together until light and fluffy.

Add the melted chocolate and beat until well incorporated. Pour the frosting in a piping bag and frost the Cupcakes.

7. Mocha Cupcakes

These Cupcakes are simply amazing. You'll get obsessed over the intense flavor of chocolate and cocoa mixed together.

Makes: 12 Cupcakes
Time: 45 min
Cupcakes

1 1/2 cups cake flour
- ¼ cup cocoa powder
- 1 ½ tsp baking powder
- ½ tsp salt
- 3/4 cup sugar
- 2 eggs
- 1/2 cup oil
- 1/2 cup buttermilk
- ½ cup hot coffee
- 1 tsp vanilla extract

Mocha buttercream

1/2 cup butter
- 2 cups powdered sugar
- 2 tbsp. whipping cream
- 1 tsp instant coffee

Directions

Preheat oven at 375 degrees. Line a cupcake tin with cupcake liners and set aside. In a big beat eggs and sugar. Beat in oil and then add buttermilk, coffee and vanilla extract. In another bowl mix flour, cocoa, baking powder, and salt. Pour the dry Ingredients to the wet Ingredients and then mix well.

Divide the batter in the cupcake forms and Bake in your preheated oven for 22-25 minutes. Let the Cupcakes cool completely before frosting them. To prepare the frosting first dissolve the coffee in the whipping cream.

Then, beat butter, sugar and whipping cream and coffee mixture together until light and fluffy. Pour the frosting in a piping bag and frost the Cupcakes.

8. Chocolate Chips Cupcakes

Chocolate chips muffins are transformed in amazing Cupcakes with a simple cream cheese frosting.

Makes: 12 Cupcakes
Time: 45 min
Ingredients
Cupcakes

1 3/4 cups cake flour
- 1 ½ tsp baking powder
- ½ tsp salt
- 3/4 cup sugar
- 2 eggs
- 1/2 cup melted butter
- 3/4 cup Greek yogurt
- 1 tsp vanilla extract
- 1 cup dark chocolate chips

Cream cheese frosting

1 cup cream cheese
- 2 cups whipping cream
- ½ cups small chocolate chips

Directions

Preheat oven at 375 degrees. Line a cupcake tin with cupcake liners and set aside. In a big beat eggs and sugar. Beat in melted butter and then add yogurt, and vanilla extract. In another bowl mix baking powder, flour, and salt. Pour the dry Ingredients to the wet Ingredients and then mix well.
Fold the chocolate chips in the batter. Divide the batter in the cupcake forms and Bake in your preheated oven for 22-25 minutes. Let the Cupcakes cool completely before frosting them. To prepare the frosting beat whipping cream with cream

cheese until stiff peaks form. Fold the mini chocolate chips. Pour the frosting in a piping bag and frost the Cupcakes.

9. Gingerbread Cupcakes

These Cupcakes make you feel it's Christmas time every time you enjoy them, due to the amazing mix of spices and a molasses touch.

Makes: 12 Cupcakes
Time: 45 min
Cupcakes

1 1/2 cups cake flour
- 1 ½ tsp baking powder
- ½ tsp salt
- 1 tsp cinnamon
- ½ tsp powdered ginger
- ¼ tsp clove
- ¼ tsp nutmeg
- 3/4 cup brown sugar
- 2 tbsp. molases
- 2 eggs

- 1/2 cup oil
- 1/2 cup buttermilk

Molasses buttercream

1/2 cup butter
- 2 cups powdered sugar
- 2 tbsp. whipping cream
- 1 tsp molases

Directions

Preheat oven at 375 degrees. Line a cupcake tin with cupcake liners and set aside. In a big beat eggs and sugar. Beat in oil and then add buttermilk, and molases. In another bowl mix flour, baking powder, cinnamon, nutmeg, clove, ginger and salt. Pour the dry Ingredients to the wet Ingredients and then mix well.
Divide the batter in the cupcake forms and Bake in your preheated oven for 22-25 minutes. Let the Cupcakes cool completely before frosting them. To prepare the frosting, beat butter, sugar and whipping cream and molases together until light and fluffy. Pour the frosting in a piping bag and frost the Cupcakes.

10. Coconut Cupcakes

These Cupcakes are full of coconut flavor coming from coconut milk and desiccated coconut. To make them even more amazing add desiccated coconut over the frosting.

Makes: 12 Cupcakes
Time: 45 min
Cupcakes

1 1/2 cups cake flour
- ½ cups desiccated coconut
- 1 ½ tsp baking powder
- ½ tsp salt
- 2 eggs
- 1 cup coconut milk full fat
- 1 tsp vanilla extract

Frosting

1/2 cup butter
- 2 cups powdered sugar
- 2 tbsp. whipping cream
- ½ cup desiccated coconut

Directions

Preheat oven at 375 degrees. Line a cupcake tin with cupcake liners and set aside. In a big beat eggs and sugar. Beat in coconut milk and vanilla extract.
In another bowl mix flour, desiccated coconut, baking powder and salt.
Pour the dry Ingredients to the wet Ingredients and then mix well.
Divide the batter in the cupcake forms and Bake in your preheated oven for 22-25 minutes. Let the Cupcakes cool completely before frosting them. To prepare the frosting, beat butter, sugar and whipping cream until light and fluffy.

Pour the frosting in a piping bag and frost the Cupcakes. Sprinkle desiccated coconut on top of each cupcake.

11. Blackberry Cupcakes

Blackberry Cupcakes are a nice twist from your usual vanilla cupcake. The blackberry touch makes them extra tasty and aromatic. Not a blackberry lover, no problem, you may replace them with your favorite berries.

Makes: 12 Cupcakes
Time: 50 min
Ingredients

Blackberry pure
- 2 cups blackberries
- ½ cup sugar
- 1 tbsp. fresh lemon juice

Cupcakes

2 cups all-purpose flour
- 2 tsp baking powder
- ½ tsp salt
- 1/2 cup yogurt
- 1/2 cup olive oil

- 1 cup sugar
- 2 eggs
- 1 tsp vanilla extract
- 4 tbsp. blackberry puree
- Zest of a lemon

Frosting

1/2 cup butter
- 2 cups powdered sugar
- 1 tbsp. cream
- 1 tsp vanilla extract
- 2 tbsp. blackberry puree

Directions

First prepare the blackberry puree. Cook the blackberries with sugar and lemon juice for 10-15 minutes, or until they're soft and have released all the juices. Remove the blackberries from heat and let them cool slightly. Puree the mixture in a food processor until very smooth. Sieve the puree and set aside. Preheat oven at 350 F. Line a cupcake tin with cupcake liners and set aside. In a big bowl beat eggs and sugar together, using a hand mixer. Add the oil, vanilla extract, blackberry puree, lemon zest and yogurt and beat well. In another bowl mix all-purpose flour, salt and baking powder. Pour the dry Ingredients to the wet Ingredients and mix just until incorporating. Divide the batter in the cupcake tin and Bake in your preheated oven for 22-25 minutes. Let the Cupcakes cool completely before frosting. While the Cupcakes are cooling prepare the frosting. In a big stand mixer mix together butter, powdered sugar, cream, blackberry puree and vanilla extract until creamy and very smooth, it may take 3-5 minutes.

Pour the frosting in a piping bag and frost the Cupcakes. Add one fresh blackberry on top Enjoy.

12. Lime Cupcakes

These Cupcakes are fresh and light. The lime curd makes them extra delicious, so don't skip it, the extra effort will be totally rewarded at the end.
Makes: 12 Cupcakes
Time: 50 min
Ingredients

Lime curd
- ½ cup sugar
- The juice and zest of 2 limes
- 2 eggs
- 1/3 cup butter

Cupcakes

1 ½ cups flour
- ½ cup butter
- ¾ cups sugar
- 2 eggs
- 1 tsp vanilla
- ½ cup milk

- ¼ tsp salt
- 2tsp baking powder
- The zest of 1 lime

Frosting

1 cup sugar
- 4 eggs whites
- 1 cup butter
- The zest of 1 lime

Directions

Start by making the lime curd. In a small pan place together all the lime curd Ingredients except for butter and cook on low heat until it gets thick and cream.
Be careful to stir the mixture all the way through, to stop the eggs from cooking.
After this sieve the lemon curd until it is still hot and beat in the butter. Cover it with cling film and put it in the fridge to cool faster.
After that, start preparing the Cupcakes. Preheat the oven at 350 F.
Line a cupcake tin with cupcake liners and set aside. In a big bowl cream butter and sugar together until soft and creamy. Then beat in the eggs until well incorporated. Add the milk and vanilla extract and mix again. In another bowl mix flour, salt, lemon zest and baking powder. Pour the dry Ingredients to the wet Ingredients and then mix well.
Divide the batter in the cupcake tin and let them bake for around 20-22 minutes.
While the Cupcakes are cooling prepare the Swiss meringue buttercream.

Place a medium sauce pan over medium heat and add the eggs and sugar. Cook it until the sugar has completely dissolved. To make sure test a small amount by rubbing it with your fingers. Once it is completely smooth, you are ready to proceed with the other steps.

Pour the eggs and sugar mixture to a stand mixer and whip until you form a glossy merengue. Start adding butter cubes and lime zest, and continue beating until well incorporated. Once the frosting is ready and the Cupcakes are cooled completely start assembling the Cupcakes. Use a small knife to cut a small hole on top of each cupcake. Fill each hole with lime curd.

13. Orange Cupcakes

Fluffy and moist orange Cupcakes frosted with an orange buttercream are the perfect winter treat.
Makes: 12 Cupcakes
Time: 50 min
Ingredients
Cupcakes

¾ cup sugar
- 1/2 cup butter
- 1 egg
- 1 tsp vanilla extract
- The juice and zest of 1 orange
- 1 ½ cups flour
- 1 ½ tsp baking powder
- ½ tsp salt

Frosting

1/2 cup butter
- 2 cups powdered sugar
- 1 tbsp. orange juice
- 1 tsp vanilla extract
- Zest of 1 orange

Directions
Preheat the oven at 375F. Prepare a cupcake pan with cupcake liners and set aside. In a medium bowl, cream the butter with sugar and then beat in the egg. Add orange juice, orange zest and vanilla extract and beat well. In another bowl mix all-purpose flour, salt, and baking powder. Pour the dry Ingredients to the wet Ingredients until well mixed.
Divide the batter on the cupcake pan. Bake for 20-22 minutes in the preheated oven. Let the Cupcakes cool completely before frosting. To prepare the frosting beat all the Ingredients together until light and fluffy.

14. Carrot Cupcakes

Imagine all the flavors and aromas of a carrot cake packed in small version. This is exactly what these carrot Cupcakes are, a miniature of a delicious and moist carrot cake with cream cheese frosting.

Makes: 12 Cupcakes
Time: 50 min
Ingredients
Cupcakes

2 cups flour
- 2 tsp baking powder
- ½ tsp salt
- 1 tsp cinnamon
- ½ tsp freshly grated nutmeg
- ½ tsp powdered ginger
- ¼ tsp powdered clove
- 1/2 cup vegetable oil
- 1 cup brown sugar
- 2 medium eggs
- ¾ cup milk
- 2 cups grated carrots
- ½ cup chopped walnuts
- ½ cup raisins
- 1/3 cup coconut

Frosting

1 cup cream cheese
- ½ cup butter
- 2 cups powdered sugar
- 1 tbsp. maple syrup
- ½ tsp cinnamon

Directions

Preheat oven at 375 F. Prepare a cupcake pan with cupcake liners and set aside. In a big bowl beat together eggs and sugar, then add oil and yogurt.
In another bowl mix all-purpose flour, salt, baking powder, cinnamon, nutmeg, ginger, clove and coconut. Mix the dry mixture with the wet mixture and then fold the grated carrot, chopped walnuts and raisins to the batter. Divide the batter in the cupcake pan and Bake in your preheated oven for 20-22 minutes. Remove from the oven and let cool completely.

Meanwhile prepare the cream cheese frosting. Beat together all the Ingredients until light, fluffy and smooth.

15. Chocolate Cherry Cupcakes

Imagine the bold flavor of dark cocoa combined with sweet flavor of cherry jam, in a single cupcake topped with cherry buttercream. Sounds like heaven to me.

Makes: 12 Cupcakes
Time: 50 min
Ingredients
Cupcakes

1 cup flour
- 1/3 cup cocoa powder
- 1 tsp baking powder
- ¼ tsp salt
- 2/3 cup sugar
- 1/3 cup oil
- 1/3 cup hot coffee
- 1/3 cup yogurt
- 1 egg
- ½ cup cherry gem

Frosting

2 cups powdered sugar
- ½ cup butter
- 2 tbsp. cherry jam

Directions

Preheat oven at 350 F.
In a big bow beat in the egg with sugar. Add the oil and yogurt and mix well. In another bowl mix flour, cocoa powder, salt and baking powder.
Mix the wet Ingredients with the dry Ingredients. Add the hot coffee and mix again. Divide the butter in the cupcake pan. Add about 1 tsp of cherry jam on each cupcake. Bake in your preheated oven for around 20-22 minutes. Let cool completely before frosting.
While the Cupcakes are frosting prepare the buttercream frosting. Beat butter and sugar together until light and fluffy. Fold in the cherry jam.
Pour the frosting in a pastry bag and frost the Cupcakes. Add a cherry on top and enjoy.

16. Raspberry Cupcakes

These Cupcakes are moist and tender, filled with raspberries and covered with a beautiful pink frosting.

Makes: 12 Cupcakes
Time: 50 min

Ingredients

Raspberry puree
- ½ cup raspberries
- 2 tbsp. sugar
- 1 tsp lemon juice

Cupcakes

1 1/2 cups cake flour
- 2 tsp baking powder
- ½ tsp salt
- Zest of 1 lemon
- ¾ cup butter
- ½ cup milk
- 2 eggs
- ¾ cup sugar
- 1 tsp vanilla extract
- 1 cup fresh raspberries

Frosting

½ cup butter
- ½ cup cream cheese
- 2 cups powdered sugar
- 3 tbsp. raspberry puree

Directions

Start by preparing the raspberry puree. In a small sauce pan place the raspberries, sugar and lemon juice and cook over medium heat for 5-10 minutes, until soft. Remove from heat and mash the raspberries with a potato masher or blender. After that prepare the raspberry muffins. Preheat the oven at 375 F. In a big bowl, cream the butter and sugar together. Add the eggs one by one and beat well. Then, add milk, vanilla extract and lemon zest. In another bowl mix flour, baking powder and salt. Add the dry mixture to the wet mixture and mix well. At the end fold the raspberries. Divide the batter in the cupcake pan and Bake in your preheated oven for 20-22 minutes. Let the Cupcakes cool completely before frosting them. To prepare the frosting just add all the Ingredients in a standing mixer and beat until light and fluffy. Pour the frosting in a piping bag and frost the Cupcakes. Enjoy with a fresh raspberry on top.

17. Grapefruit Poppy Seeds Cupcakes

These one of a kind Cupcakes are bitter-sweet, and so light and tender. Poppy seeds add such a nice crunch and the cream cheese frosting matches perfectly with the cake base.
Makes: 12 Cupcakes
Time: 50 min
Ingredients

Grapefruit juice
- ½ cup fresh grapefruit juice
- 2 tbsp. sugar

Cupcakes

1 ¾ cup cake flour
- ½ tsp salt
- 1 ½ tsp baking powder
- ½ tsp baking soda
- 1 ½ tbsp. poppy seeds
- Zest of 1 grapefruit
- ½ cup butter
- ¾ cup sugar
- ½ cup fresh grapefruit juice
- 2 eggs
- ½ cup yogurt

Frosting

½ cup butter
- ½ cup cream cheese
- 2 cups powdered sugar

Directions

Start by preparing the grapefruit syrup. In a small saucepan boil together grapefruit juice and sugar, until the juice starts to thicken a bit. Remove from heat and strain it to make sure there is no pulp left.

Now, start preparing the Cupcakes. Preheat oven at 350 F. Prepare a cupcake pan with cupcake liners. In a big bowl, cream together sugar and butter. Add the eggs and beat well. Then, add yogurt and grapefruit juice and zest and mix again.

In another bowl, mix together the flour, baking soda, baking powder, poppy seeds and salt. Pour in the dry Ingredients to the wet ingredient and mix well. Divide the batter in the cupcake pan and Bake in your preheated oven for 22-25 minutes. Once they are perfectly baked remove from the oven and drizzle a little bit syrup over each cupcake. Let the Cupcakes cool completely before frosting them. To prepare the frosting beat all the Ingredients together until light and fluffy.

18. Lemon And Poppy Seeds Cupcakes

Lemon and poppy seeds are made for each other. They match perfectly on lemon cake, poppy seeds lemon curd and also on this amazing poppy seeds Cupcakes.
Makes: 12 Cupcakes
Time: 50 min
Ingredients
Cupcakes

1 ¾ cup cake flour
- ½ tsp salt
- 1 ½ tsp baking powder
- ½ tsp baking soda

- 1 ½ tbsp. poppy seeds
- Zest of 1 lemon
- ½ cup olive oil
- 1 cup sugar
- ½ cup fresh grapefruit juice
- 2 eggs
- ½ cup yogurt

Frosting

1 cup cream cheese
- 2 cups sweetened whipping cream
- Zest of 1 lemon

Directions

Start by preparing the Cupcakes. Preheat oven at 350 F. Prepare a cupcake pan with cupcake liners. In a big bowl cream together eggs and sugar. Add the olive oil and beat well. Then, add yogurt and lemon juice and zest and mix again. In another bowl mix together flour, poppy seeds, baking powder, baking soda and salt. Pour the dry Ingredients to the wet ingredient and mix well. Divide the batter in the cupcake pan and Bake in your preheated oven for 22-25 minutes. Let the Cupcakes cool completely before frosting them. To prepare the frosting beat all the Ingredients together until light and fluffy.

19. Apple Cupcakes

These Cupcakes bring the best of fall flavors together, starting with apple and cinnamon and ending with a touch of caramel.

Makes: 12 Cupcakes
Time: 50 min
Ingredients
Cupcakes

1 cup flour
- ¾ cup oatmeal flour
- ½ tsp salt
- 1 ½ tsp baking powder
- ½ tsp baking soda
- 1 tsp cinnamon
- ½ tsp grated nutmeg
- ½ cup canola oil
- 1 cup brown sugar
- 2 eggs
- ½ cup milk
- 2 medium apples cored and cut into cubes

Frosting

½ cup butter
- ½ cup cream cheese

- 2 cups powdered sugar
- ½ tsp cinnamon
- ¼ cup thick caramel sauce

Directions

Start by preparing the **Cupcakes**. Preheat oven at 350 F. Prepare a cupcake pan with cupcake liners. In a big bowl cream together eggs and sugar. Add the canola oil and beat well. Then, add milk and mix again. In another bowl mix together flour, baking powder, baking soda, cinnamon, nutmeg and salt. Pour the dry Ingredients to the wet ingredient and mix well. Fold the apple cubes in batter. Divide the batter in the cupcake pan and Bake in your preheated oven for 22-25 minutes. Let the Cupcakes cool completely before frosting them. To prepare the frosting beat all the Ingredients together except for the caramel sauce, until light and fluffy. At the end fold the caramel sauce in the frosting. Pour the frosting in the piping bag and frost the Cupcakes.

20. Peach Cupcakes

These Cupcakes are filled with peach flavor, which comes from fresh and ripe peaches and peach jam. To make them even more peachy top them with a peach buttercream.

Makes: 12 Cupcakes
Time: 50 min

Ingredients

Cupcakes

1 cup flour
- ¾ cup whole wheat flour
- ½ tsp salt
- 1 ½ tsp baking powder
- ½ tsp baking soda
- 1 tsp cinnamon
- ½ cup canola oil
- ½ cup brown sugar
- 2 eggs
- ½ cup milk
- ½ cup peach jam
- 2 medium peached cored and cut into cubes

Frosting

½ cup butter
- 2 cups powdered sugar
- ¼ cup thick peach jam

Directions

Start by preparing the Cupcakes. Preheat oven at 350 F. Prepare a cupcake pan with cupcake liners. In a big bowl cream together eggs and sugar. Add the canola oil and beat well. Then, add milk and peach jam and mix again. In another bowl mix together flour, baking powder, baking soda, cinnamon and salt.

Pour the dry Ingredients to the wet ingredient and mix well. Fold the peach cubes in batter. Divide the batter in the cupcake pan and Bake in your preheated oven for 22-25 minutes. Let the Cupcakes cool completely before frosting them. To prepare the frosting beat all the Ingredients together except for the peach jam, until light and fluffy. At the end fold the peach jam in the frosting. Pour the frosting in the piping bag and frost the Cupcakes.

21. Triple Berry Cupcakes

How can a blueberry cupcake get better? Just add strawberries. How can it get even better? Add raspberries.
Makes: 12 Cupcakes
Time: 50 min
Ingredients
Cupcakes

1 1/2 cups cake flour
- ½ tsp salt
- 2 tsp baking powder
- 1 tsp vanilla extract
- ¾ cup butter
- ¾ cup sugar

- Zest of 1 lemon
- 2 eggs
- ¾ cup buttermilk
- ½ cup peach jam
- 2 cups of mixed berries (strawberries, blueberries, raspberries)

Frosting

½ cup butter
- 1 cup cream cheese
- 2 cups powdered sugar

Directions

Start by preparing the Cupcakes. Preheat oven at 350 F. Prepare a cupcake pan with cupcake liners. In a big bowl, cream together butter and sugar. Add the eggs and beat well. Then, add buttermilk and vanilla extract and mix again. In another bowl mix together flour, baking powder, lemon zest and salt.
Pour the dry Ingredients to the wet ingredient and mix well. Fold the berries in batter. Divide the batter in the cupcake pan and Bake in your preheated oven for 22-25 minutes. Let the Cupcakes cool completely before frosting them. To prepare the frosting beat all the Ingredients together until light and fluffy.
Pour the frosting in the piping bag and frost the Cupcakes. Don't forget to add some fresh berries on top.

22. Tropical Mango Cupcakes

These Cupcakes are packed full of tropical flavor. Take one of them, close your eyes, bite it and imagine yourself at a beautiful beach with coconut and palm trees.

Makes: 12 Cupcakes
Time: 50 min

Ingredients
Cupcakes

1 1/2 cups cake flour
- ½ tsp salt
- 2 tsp baking powder
- 1 tsp vanilla extract
- 1/4 cup butter
- 1 cup sugar
- 2 eggs
- ¾ cup coconut milk

Frosting

¾ cup unsalted butter
- 3 cups powdered sugar
- ½ mango peeled and cut into cubes

Directions
Start by preparing the Cupcakes.
Preheat oven at 350 F.
Prepare a cupcake pan with cupcake liners.

In a big bowl, cream together butter and sugar. Add the eggs and beat well. Then, add coconut milk and vanilla extract and mix again. In another bowl mix together flour, baking powder and salt. Pour the dry Ingredients to the wet ingredient and mix well. Divide the batter in the cupcake pan and Bake in your preheated oven for 22-25 minutes. Let the Cupcakes cool completely before frosting them. To prepare the frosting beat all the Ingredients together except for the mango cubes until light and fluffy. Fold the mango cubes in the frosting. Pour the frosting in the piping bag and frost the Cupcakes. Don't forget to add some desiccated coconut on top.

23. Banana And Nut Cupcakes With Ricotta And Honey Frosting

Banana makes these Cupcakes so soft and moist, cinnamon adds that extra earthy flavor and spicy touch and ricotta and honey make the perfect healthy frosting.
Makes: 12 Cupcakes
Time: 50 min
Ingredients
Cupcakes

1 1/2 cups cake flour
- 2 tsp baking powder
- ½ tsp salt
- 1 tsp cinnamon
- ½ cup canola oil
- ½ cup milk
- 2 very ripe bananas mashed
- 2 eggs
- ¾ cup brown sugar
- 1 cup chopped walnuts

Frosting
- 1 cup ricotta
- 1/3 cup honey

Directions
Start by preparing the Cupcakes. Preheat oven at 350 F. Prepare a cupcake pan with cupcake liners. In a big bowl beat together eggs and sugar. Add the oil, milk and mashed bananas and mix well. In another bowl mix together flour, cinnamon, baking powder and salt. At the and fold in the nuts. Pour the dry Ingredients to the wet Ingredients and then mix well.
Divide the batter in the cupcake pan and Bake in your preheated oven for 22-25 minutes. Let the Cupcakes cool completely before frosting them. To prepare the frosting ricotta with honey very well. Pour the frosting in the piping bag and frost the Cupcakes. Don't forget to add some chopped nuts on top.

24. Strawberry Cupcakes

Have you ever thought to match strawberries with white chocolate? If not, it is a must try. They pair perfectly on these smoothies too.

Makes: 12 Cupcakes
Time: 50 min
Ingredients
Cupcakes

1 1/2 cups cake flour
- 2 tsp baking powder
- ½ tsp salt
- 1 tsp vanilla extract
- ¾ cup batter at room temperature
- ½ cup buttermilk
- 1 cup chopped strawberries
- 2 eggs
- ¾ cup sugar
- 1 cup white chocolate chips

Frosting

1/2 cup butter
- 1 cup cream cheese
- 2 cups powdered sugar
- 1/3 cup strawberry jam

Directions

Start by preparing the Cupcakes. Preheat oven at 350 F. Prepare a cupcake pan with cupcake liners. In a big bowl, cream together butter and sugar. Add the eggs, milk and vanilla extract and mix well. In another bowl mix together flour, baking powder and salt. Pour the dry Ingredients to the wet Ingredients and then mix well.
At the and fold in the chopped strawberries and white

chocolate chips. Divide the batter in the cupcake pan and Bake in your preheated oven for 22-25 minutes. Let the Cupcakes cool completely before frosting them. To prepare the frosting beat all the Ingredients together until light and fluffy. Pour the frosting in the piping bag and frost the Cupcakes. Don't forget to add a fresh strawberry on top.

25. Blueberry And Oatmeal Cupcakes

Fresh and juicy blueberries meet oatmeal and olive oil on these delicious Cupcakes.
Makes: 12 Cupcakes
Time: 50 min
Ingredients
Cupcakes

1 cup whole wheat flour
- 1 ½ cups old-fashioned oatmeal
- A pinch of salt
- The zest of 1 medium lemon
- 2 tsp baking powder
- 1 cup brown sugar

- ½ cup olive oil
- 3 eggs
- ½ cup buttermilk
- 1 cup fresh blueberries

Frosting

1 cup cream cheese
- 2 cups sweetened whipping cream
- 1/4 cup blueberry jam

Directions

Start by preparing the Cupcakes. Preheat oven at 350 F. Prepare a cupcake pan with cupcake liners.
In a big bowl beat together eggs and sugar. Add the oil, buttermilk, lemon zest and vanilla extract and mix well.
In another bowl mix together flour, oatmeal baking powder and salt.
Pour the dry Ingredients to the wet Ingredients and then mix well.
At the end, fold in blueberries. Divide the batter in the cupcake pan and Bake in your preheated oven for 22-25 minutes. Let the Cupcakes cool completely before frosting them. To prepare the frosting beat cream cheese and whipping cream until light and fluffy. Fold the blueberry jam in the frosting.
Pour the frosting in the piping bag and frost the Cupcakes. Don't forget to add a fresh strawberry on top.

26. Pear And Chocolate Cupcakes

When pears marry chocolate, in a cupcake a beautiful and so flavorful love child is born.

Makes: 12 Cupcakes
Time: 50 min

Ingredients
Cupcakes

1 ¼ cup whole wheat flour
- ½ cup cocoa
- ½ tsp salt
- 2 tsp baking powder
- ½ cup butter, room temperature
- 1 cup brown sugar
- 2 medium eggs
- ½ cup buttermilk
- 1 tsp vanilla extract
- 2 medium pears cut in cubes

Frosting

1/2 cup butter
- 2 cups cream cheese
- 1 tsp vanilla extract

Directions
Start by preparing the Cupcakes.
Preheat oven at 350 F.

Prepare a cupcake pan with cupcake liners. In a big bowl, beat together sugar and butter. Add the eggs, buttermilk, and vanilla extract and mix well. In another bowl mix together the cocoa baking powder, flour and salt.
Pour the dry Ingredients to the wet Ingredients and then mix well.
At the end, fold in pear cubes. Divide the batter in the cupcake pan and Bake in your preheated oven for 22-25 minutes. Let the Cupcakes cool completely before frosting them. To prepare the frosting cream butter and sugar together until light and fluffy. Pour the frosting in the piping bag and frost the Cupcakes.

27. All Maple Cupcakes

Moist and tender, with a nice brown colour and caramel taste, this maple Cupcakes will soon become your favourites. To go the extra mile, sweeten the cream cheese with maple syrup, for a healthy and so delicious touch.

Makes: 12 Cupcakes
Time: 45 min
Ingredients

Maple Cupcakes
- 1 ½ all-purpose flour
- ½ tsp salt
- 1 ½ tsp baking powder
- 1 stick soft butter
- ¾ cup maple syrup
- 2 eggs
- ¾ cup milk
- ½ cup toasted and chopped hazelnuts

Maple cream cheese frosting

8 ounces cream cheese
- ½ stick soft butter
- 2 tbsp. maple syrup

Directions
Preheat the oven at 375 F and line a cupcake tin with baking papers.
In a big bowl, cream the butter and sugar and beat in the eggs one by one. Cream well and then add the milk and the maple syrup. In another bowl, mix flour, salt and baking paper. Add the dry Ingredients to the wet Ingredients and then mix well.
Divide the batter in the cupcake tin and Bake in your preheated oven for around 20-25 minutes. Let the Cupcakes cool completely, then start preparing the frosting.
Beat together, cream cheese, butter and maple syrup. Pour the frosting in a pastry bag and frost the Cupcakes.

28. Peanut Butter Cupcakes

These Cupcakes are a must try, for all peanut butter fans. They burst with peanut butter flavor coming from both cake and frosting.

Makes: 12 Cupcakes
Time: 50 minutes
Ingredients
Cupcakes

1 ½ all-purpose flour
- ½ cup soft butter
- 1 ½ tsp of baking powder
- ½ tsp salt
- ½ cup peanut butter
- 1 cup brown sugar
- 2 eggs
- ¾ cup buttermilk
- ½ cup toasted peanuts

Frosting

½ cup butter
- 2 cups powdered sugar
- ¼ cup peanut butter

Directions
Preheat the oven at 375 F and line a cupcake tin with baking papers.
In a big bowl, cream the butter, peanut butter and sugar and beat in the eggs one by one.
Add the buttermilk and mix well.
In another bowl, mix flour, salt and baking paper.
Add the dry Ingredients to the wet Ingredients and then mix well.
Fold the peanuts in the batter.
Divide the batter in the cupcake tin and Bake in your preheated oven for around 20-25 minutes.
Let the Cupcakes cool completely, and then start preparing the frosting.
Beat together, butter, peanut butter and sugar until light and fluffy. Pour the frosting in a pastry bag and frost the Cupcakes.

29. Liquor Buttercream Cupcakes

These are grown up Cupcakes which get their unique touch by the liquor added in the buttercream and cake batter.
Makes: 12 Cupcakes
Time: 45 min

Ingredients
Cupcakes

1 3/4 all-purpose flour
- ½ tsp salt
- 2 tsp baking powder
- 3/4 cup soft butter
- ½ cup chocolate chips
- 2 eggs
- ¾ cup milk
- ¾ cup brown sugar
- 4 tbsp. cram liquor

Frosting

½ cup butter
- 2 cups powdered sugar
- 2 tbsp. cream liquor

Directions

Preheat the oven at 375 F and line a cupcake tin with baking papers.
Melt the chocolate in a double boiler or microwave and set aside.
In a big bowl, cream the butter, and sugar and beat in the eggs one by one.
Add the milk and liquor and mix well.
In another bowl, mix flour, salt and baking paper.
Add the dry Ingredients to the wet Ingredients and then mix well.
Add the chocolate in the batter and mix well.
Divide the batter in the cupcake tin and Bake in your preheated oven for around 20-25 minutes.
Let the Cupcakes cool completely, and then start preparing the frosting.

Beat together, butter, liquor and sugar until light and fluffy. Pour the frosting in a pastry bag and frost the Cupcakes.

30. Chocolate And Peanut Butter Cupcakes

Dense, moist, chocolaty with a strong touch of peanut butter, these Cupcakes are luscious and heavy, but totally worth all the calories.

Makes: 12 Cupcakes
Time: 50 min
Ingredients
Cupcakes

1 ½ all-purpose flour
- ½ tsp salt
- 1 ½ tsp baking powder
- 1/4 cup cocoa powder
- ½ cup soft butter
- ½ cup peanut butter
- 1 cup brown sugar
- 3 eggs
- 1/2 cup buttermilk

Frosting

½ cup butter
- 2 cups powdered sugar

- ¼ cup peanut butter
- 2 tbsp. unsweetened cocoa powder

Directions

Preheat the oven at 375 F and line a cupcake tin with baking papers.

In a big bowl, cream the butter, peanut butter and sugar and beat in the eggs one by one. Add the buttermilk and mix well.

In another bowl, mix flour, cocoa, salt and baking paper. Add the dry Ingredients to the wet Ingredients and then mix well.

Divide the batter in the cupcake tin and Bake in your preheated oven for around 20-25 minutes.

Let the Cupcakes cool completely, and then start preparing the frosting.

Beat together, butter, peanut butter, cocoa powder and sugar until light and fluffy. Pour the frosting in a pastry bag and frost the Cupcakes.

Conclusion

A great cupcake is a work of art and has the power to make every situation better and every person smile. The beauty of it, is that they are portion sized, so no need to make a mess cutting them and can play with buttercream flavors, to satisfy everyone's taste.

Part 2

Introduction

Cupcakes recipes are easy to understand and quick to make. You only need the correct measurements to start baking. Most people do not realize, but baking is the easiest above all the cooking matters since you only need the right directions, and you will be able to make the best cupcake recipes to serve your friends and family.

If you are a mother, then this book would prove to be the best guide to start baking for your family. By the end of this book, you will be a pro at cupcakes at your very own home. These recipes are enough for you to make different flavored cupcakes for almost a month! So what are you waiting for? Let's get started!

Learn About Sweetness In Life

We think that desserts are unhealthy and they will only increase our weight. Well, that is just a misconception because the latest research has concluded that having desserts can help you stay active and keeps your immune system strong as well. It reduces the risk of heart diseases and is beneficial in many ways but this is all depending on the ingredients we use in our recipes as well.

Desserts play a big role in the happiness or as appreciation in someone's life. Whenever we hear good news, we prefer to have desserts. Here are some of the amazing benefits of desserts and why you should try to make then often.

1. Healthy

Whenever we crave for something, it is because we are lacking the nutrients which consist in that food which we crave for. We need low carb nutrients in our body which are the carbohydrates to keep the body healthy. Desserts aren't the healthiest form of carbohydrates for the body but if you are craving too much for it then you should have it once in a while without overthinking. The recipes with dark chocolate are rich in fiber, vitamin, antioxidants and more. It helps you keep the digestive system strong and you tend to stay more energetic.

2. Brings Pleasure

You must have felt that whenever you have a dessert, you feel happy all of a sudden? It produces the necessary carbohydrates in the body which helps the brain in producing chemicals such as serotonin activating the emotional well-being of humans. You start taking things positive and enjoy the life once again. It is like a treat for your brain and body which will help you release stress.

3. Fruit Cupcakes

Most of the desserts are made of fruits so if you are someone who does not like to have raw fruits then desserts could be the best way to consume fruits. We need fruits to fulfill the essential nutrients which sometimes it can be lacking in some other foods that we have daily. So try to have fruity desserts which will provide you with additional nutrients that might be missing in your body to sustain a healthy lifestyle.

When you add raspberries or strawberries, they are rich in protein and healthy fats for your body. So taking fruits in the daily diet is vital and essential to keep the brain and body active in many ways. When you combine it with other ingredients, the nutrient level of the fruit increases and proves to be healthier for you so if you are missing on fruits, you can get it in the desserts!

Chapter 1: Delicious Fruity Cupcakes

Recipe 01: Raspberries Cupcakes

Cooking time: 15 minutes

Servings: 2

Description: Get started with these amazing raspberries cupcakes recipe to enjoy it this evening!

Ingredients:

- Butter – 1 cup
- Caster sugar – 1 cup
- Vanilla essence – 1 tbsp.
- Eggs – 2
- Flour – 1 cup
- Milk – ½ cup
- Raspberries (frozen) – 1 cup

Icing:

- Icing sugar – 1 cup
- Butter – 1 cup

- Raspberries (frozen) – ½ cup
- Pistachios to garnish

Directions:
1. Add butter into the bowl.
2. Mix caster sugar, vanilla essence, eggs, flour and milk with raspberries.
3. Heat the oven to 350 F and prepare the muffin tins.
4. Insert paper cases. Pour the batter into the paper cases.
5. Bake for 15 minutes.
6. Meanwhile, prepare the icing: Mix icing sugar, butter and raspberries into the bowl.
7. When cupcakes are ready, spread the icing on top of it with sprinkling pistachio.
8. Serve when ready!

Recipe 02: Orange Flavored Cupcakes

Cooking time: 15 minutes

Servings: 2

Description: Love oranges? Here is the best recipe for you to try!

Ingredients:

- Flour – 2 cups
- Caster sugar – 1 cup
- Milk – 1 cup
- Butter – 1 cup
- Eggs – 2
- Vanilla essence – 1 tbsp.
- Oranges juice – ½ cup

Icing:

- Icing sugar – 1 cup
- Orange rind (grated) – 1
- Cream – 1 cup

Directions:
1. Add flour into the bowl.
2. Mix caster sugar, milk, butter, eggs, vanilla essence and orange juice.
3. Heat the oven to 350 F and prepare the muffin tins.
4. Insert paper cases. Pour the batter into the paper cases.
5. Bake for 15 minutes.
6. Meanwhile, prepare **Icing:** mix icing sugar, orange rind and cream into the bowl.
7. When ready, spread the icing on cupcakes to serve!

Recipe 03: Vanilla Bean Cupcakes

Cooking time: 15 minutes

Servings: 2

Description: Try the vanilla bean cupcakes and you won't be able get over it!

Ingredients:

- Butter – 1 cup
- Caster sugar – 2 tbsp.
- Vanilla bean paste – 1 tbsp.
- Eggs – 2
- Flour – 2 cups
- Milk – 2 cups

Butter Icing:

- Butter – 2 cups

- Icing sugar – 1 cup
- Milk – ½ cup

Directions:
1. Add butter into the bowl.
2. Mix caster sugar, vanilla bean, eggs, flour and milk.
3. Heat the oven to 350 F and prepare the muffin tins.
4. Insert paper cases. Pour the batter into the paper cases.
5. Bake for 15 minutes.
6. Meanwhile, prepare the Icing: mix butter, icing sugar and milk into the bowl.
7. When ready, spread the icing on cupcakes to serve!

Recipe 04: Strawberry Jam Cupcakes

Cooking time: 15 minutes

Servings: 2

Description: You will love the taste of strawberry jam in this recipe so do not miss out on this one!

Ingredients:
- Cupcake powder – 1 pack
- Milk – 2 cups
- Strawberries (chopped) – 1 cup
- Cream cheese – 2 cups
- Icing sugar – 2 tbsp.
- Strawberry jam – 2 tbsp.

Directions:
1. Add cupcake powder into the bowl.
2. Mix milk and strawberries.
3. Heat the oven to 350 F and prepare the muffin tins.
4. Insert paper cases. Pour the batter into the paper cases.

5. Bake for 15 minutes.
6. Meanwhile mix icing sugar and cream cheese with strawberry jam.
7. When ready, spread icing on cupcakes to serve!

Recipe 05: Buttermilk Cupcakes

Cooking time: 15 minutes

Servings: 2

Description: Try these soft and delicious buttermilk cupcakes recipe tonight!

Ingredients:

- Flour – 2 cups
- Baking powder – 2 tbsp.
- Bicarbonate soda – 2 tbsp.
- Banana (mashed) – 2
- Banana slices – 8
- Caster sugar – 2 cups
- Butter – 2 cups
- Buttermilk – 2 cups
- Eggs – 2

Directions:

1. Add flour into the bowl.
2. Mix baking powder, soda, banana, banana slices, caster sugar, butter, buttermilk and eggs.
3. Heat the oven to 350 F and prepare the muffin tins.
4. Insert paper cases. Pour the batter into the paper cases.
5. Bake for 15 minutes.
6. When ready, serve and enjoy!

Chapter 2: Delicious Flavors Of Cupcakes

Recipe 06: Chocolate Cupcakes

Cooking time: 15 minutes
Servings: 2
Description: Love chocolate? Here is the best simple chocolate cupcake recipe for you!
Ingredients:

- Butter – 2 cups
- White chocolate – 2 cups
- Caster sugar – 2 cups
- Milk – 1 cup
- Eggs – 2
- Flour – 2 cups
- Chocolate (chopped) – 1 cup
- Chocolate topping – to drizzle

Directions:
1. Add butter into the bowl.
2. Mix white chocolate, caster sugar, milk, eggs, flour and chocolate into the bowl.
3. Heat the oven to 350 F and prepare the muffin tins.
4. Insert paper cases. Pour the batter into the paper cases.
5. Bake for 15 minutes.
6. When ready, add chocolate topping to serve!

Recipe 07: Jelly Bean Cupcakes

Cooking time: 15 minutes

Servings: 2

Description: For the love of jelly beans, try this amazing cupcake recipe today!

Ingredients:

- Butter – 2 cups
- Vanilla extract – 2 tbsp.
- Caster sugar – 2 tbsp.
- Eggs – 2
- Flour – 2 cups
- Pink food color – 2 tbsp.
- Jelly beans to decorate

Icing:

- Butter – 2 cups
- Icing sugar – 2 tbsp.
- Milk – 1 cup

Directions:
1. Add butter into the bowl.

2. Mix vanilla extract, caster sugar, eggs, flour and pink food color.
3. Heat the oven to 350 F and prepare the muffin tins.
4. Insert paper cases. Pour the batter into the paper cases.
5. Bake for 15 minutes.
6. Meanwhile, prepare the **Icing:** mix butter, icing sugar and milk into the bowl.
7. When ready, spread the icing and place jelly beans on top to serve!

Recipe 08: Maltesers Cupcakes

Cooking time: 15 minutes

Servings: 2

Description: This recipe is for those maltesers lovers out there!

Ingredients:

- Butter – 2 cups
- Dark chocolate – 2 cups
- Water – ½ cup
- Instant coffee – 2 tbsp.
- Brown sugar – 2 cups
- Flour – 2 cups
- Cocoa powder – 1 tbsp.
- Egg – 2
- Maltesers for decoration

Frosting:

- Butter – 2 cups
- Icing sugar – 2 tbsp.

- Milk – 2 cups

Directions:
1. Add butter into the bowl.
2. Mix dark chocolate, water, instant coffee, brown sugar, flour, cocoa powder and egg.
3. Heat the oven to 350 F and prepare the muffin tins.
4. Insert paper cases. Pour the batter into the paper cases.
5. Bake for 15 minutes.
6. Meanwhile, prepare frosting: mix butter, icing sugar and milk into the bowl.
7. When ready, spread the frosting on cupcakes with maltesers on top to serve!

Recipe 09: Coffee Flavored Cupcakes

Cooking time: 15 minutes

Servings: 2

Description: Try the amazing coffee cupcakes to enjoy with the tea this evening!

Ingredients:
- Butter – 2 cups
- Vanilla extract – 2 tbsp.
- Caster sugar – 2 cups
- Eggs – 2
- Flour – 2 cups
- Milk – 2 cups
- Cocoa powder – 2 tbsp.

Icing:
- Butter – 2 cups
- Icing sugar – 1 cup

- Coffee essence – 1 tbsp.
- Chocolate sprinkles to decorate

Directions:
1. Add butter into the bowl.
2. Mix vanilla extract, caster sugar, eggs, flour, milk and cocoa powder.
3. Heat the oven to 350 F and prepare the muffin tins.
4. Insert paper cases. Pour the batter into the paper cases.
5. Bake for 15 minutes.
6. Meanwhile, mix butter, icing sugar and coffee essence into the bowl.
7. When ready, spread the icing with sprinkling chocolate to serve!

Recipe 10: Pink Coconut Cupcakes

Cooking time: 15 minutes

Servings: 2

Description: If you are concerned with your daily sugar intake, then keep in mind that you can adjust the sweetness to your own liking.

Ingredients:

- Butter – 2 cups
- Caster sugar – 2 tbsp.
- Vanilla essence – 2 tbsp.
- Eggs – 2
- Flour – 2 cups
- Milk – 2 cups
- Water – 1 cup
- Vanilla essence – 1 tbsp.

- Pink food color – 2 drops
- Coconut (shredded) – 2 cups

Directions:
1. Add butter into the bowl.
2. Mix caster sugar, vanilla essence, eggs, milk, flour, water, caster sugar, vanilla essence and pink food color.
3. Heat the oven to 350 F and prepare the muffin tins.
4. Insert paper cases. Pour the batter into the paper cases.
5. Bake for 15 minutes.
6. When ready, sprinkle coconut to serve!

Recipe 11: Cocoa Cupcakes

Cooking time: 15 minutes

Servings: 2

Description: Once you try these cocoa cupcakes, you will surely fall in love with it!

Ingredients:

- White chocolate – 1 cup
- Dark chocolate – 1 cup
- Milk – 2 cups
- Vanilla extract – 2 tbsp.
- Butter – 2 cups
- Water – 1 cup
- Instant coffee – 1 tbsp.
- Eggs – 2
- Flour – 2 cups
- Icing sugar – 2 cups
- Cocoa to dust

Directions:
1. Add milk into the bowl.
2. Mix white chocolate, dark chocolate, vanilla extract, butter, water, instant coffee, eggs and flour.
3. Heat the oven to 350 F and prepare the muffin tins.
4. Insert paper cases. Pour the batter into the paper cases.
5. Bake for 15 minutes.
6. When ready, dust cocoa and icing sugar to serve!

Recipe 12: Dark Chocolate Cupcakes

Cooking time: 15 minutes

Servings: 2

Description: I am a big fan of dark chocolate and I'm sure you will love it too! Just the right amount of bitter sweet.

Ingredients:

- Dark chocolate – 2 cups
- Water – 1 cup
- Butter – 2 cups
- Brown sugar – 2 cups
- Eggs – 3
- Flour – 2 cups
- Cocoa powder – 2 tbsp.

Icing:

- Dark chocolate – 2 cups
- Sour cream – 2 cups

Directions:
1. Add butter into the bowl.
2. Mix dark chocolate, water, brown sugar, eggs, flour and cocoa powder.

3. Heat the oven to 350 F and prepare the muffin tins.
4. Insert paper cases. Pour the batter into the paper cases.
5. Bake for 15 minutes.
6. Meanwhile, prepare the **Icing:** mix dark chocolate and sour cream into the bowl.
7. When ready, spread the icing on cupcakes to serve!

Recipe 13: Pumpkin Cupcakes

Cooking time: 15 minutes

Servings: 2

Description: Try the tasty pumpkins flavored cupcakes recipe at home tonight with this amazing recipe!

Ingredients:

- Butter – 2 cups
- Brown sugar – 2 tbsp.
- Eggs – 2
- Pumpkin (mashed) – 2 cups
- Flour – 2 cups
- Milk – 1 cup
- Ground cinnamon – 2 tbsp.
- Ground ginger – ½ tbsp.
- Cream cheese – 2 cups
- Caster sugar – 2 tbsp.
- Red food color – 2 drops
- Yellow food color – 2 drops
- Caramel topping to serve
- Pecans (chopped) to serve

Directions:

1. Add butter into the bowl.
2. Mix brown sugar, eggs, pumpkin, flour, milk, cinnamon, ginger, cream cheese, caster sugar, red food color and yellow food color.
3. Heat the oven to 350 F and prepare the muffin tins.
4. Insert paper cases. Pour the batter into the paper cases.
5. Bake for 15 minutes.
6. When ready, spread caramel and sprinkle pecans to serve!

Chapter 3: Soft And Sweet Cupcakes

Recipe 14: Caramel Cupcakes

Cooking time: 15 minutes

Servings: 2

Description: An amazing recipe of caramel cupcake which you should definitely try!

Ingredients:

- Cupcakes powder – 1 pack
- Milk – 2 cups
- Brown sugar – 2 cups
- Caramel – 1 cup
- Icing sugar – 2 cups

Directions:

1. Add cupcakes powder into the bowl.
2. Mix brown sugar, milk, caramel and icing sugar.
3. Heat the oven to 350 F and prepare the muffin tins.
4. Insert paper cases. Pour the batter into the paper cases.
5. Bake for 15 minutes.

6. When ready, serve!

Recipe 15: Almond Meal Cupcakes

Cooking time: 15 minutes

Servings: 2

Description: Try the amazing almond flavored cupcakes where I guarantee that you would want to have it every day!

Ingredients:

- Butter – 2 cups
- Caster sugar – 2 tbsp.
- Eggs – 2
- Flour – 2 cups
- Almond meal – 2 tbsp.
- Milk – 1 cup
- Cream – 2 cups

Icing:

- Orange juice – 3 tbsp.
- Caster sugar – 2 tbsp.
- Orange – 1

Directions:
1. Add butter into the bowl.
2. Mix caster sugar, eggs, flour, almond meal, milk and cream.
3. Heat the oven to 350 F and prepare the muffin tins.
4. Insert paper cases. Pour the batter into the paper cases.
5. Bake for 15 minutes.
6. Meanwhile, prepare the **Icing:** mix orange juice, orange and caster sugar into the bowl.
7. When ready, spread the icing on cupcakes to serve!

Recipe 16: Lemon Zest Cupcake

Cooking time: 15 minutes

Servings: 2

Description: This lemon cupcake recipe is the perfect dessert to have when you need that extra boost of energy during the day!

Ingredients:

- Butter – 2 cups
- Caster sugar – 2 cups
- Eggs – 2
- Lemon zest – 2 tbsp.
- Lemon juice – 2 tbsp.
- Flour – 2 cups
- Baking powder – 1 tbsp.
- Yogurt – 2 cups
- Icing sugar – 2 tbsp.
- Berries to garnish

Directions:
1. Add butter into the bowl.
2. Mix caster sugar, eggs, lemon zest, lemon juice, flour, baking powder and yogurt.
3. Heat the oven to 350 F and prepare the muffin tins.
4. Insert paper cases. Pour the batter into the paper cases.
5. Bake for 15 minutes.
6. When ready, sprinkle icing sugar and garnish berries.

Recipe 17: Sour Cream Mix Cupcake

Cooking time: 15 minutes

Servings: 2

Description: Make sure to try this combination of sweet cupcake with sour cream. You will surely love it!

Ingredients:

- Butter – 2 cups
- Caster sugar – 2 tbsp.
- Eggs – 2
- Flour – 2 cups
- Almond meal – ½ cup
- Sour cream – 2 cups
- Icing flowers – 1 cup

Icing:

- Icing sugar – 2 cups
- Butter – 2 cups
- Water – 1 cup
- Pink food color – 2 drops

Directions:
1. Add butter into the bowl.
2. Mix caster sugar, eggs, flour, almond meal and sour cream.
3. Heat the oven to 350 F and prepare the muffin tins.
4. Insert paper cases. Pour the batter into the paper cases.
5. Bake for 15 minutes.
6. Meanwhile, prepare the Icing: mix icing sugar, butter, and water with food color.
7. When ready, spread the icing with decorating each cupcake with flowers to serve!

Recipe 18: Lime And Coconut Cupcake

Cooking time: 15 minutes

Servings: 2

Description: Amazing lime and coconut cupcakes you would want to try at home!

Ingredients:

- Flour – 2 cups
- Baking powder – 2 tbsp.
- Caster sugar – 1 cup
- Butter – 2 cups
- Eggs – 2
- Coconut milk – 2 cups
- Lime zest – 1 tbsp.
- Coconut (shredded) – 2 cups

Icing:

- Lime zest – 2 tbsp.
- Egg whites – 2
- Caster sugar – 1 tbsp.

Directions:
1. Add flour into the bowl.
2. Mix baking powder, caster sugar, butter, eggs, coconut milk and lemon zest.
3. Heat the oven to 350 F and prepare the muffin tins.
4. Insert paper cases. Pour the batter into the paper cases.
5. Bake for 15 minutes.
6. Meanwhile prepare the **Icing:** mix lime zest, egg whites and caster sugar.
7. When ready, spread the icing with sprinkling coconut to serve!

Recipe 19: Cream Cheese Devil Cupcakes

Cooking time: 15 minutes

Servings: 2

Description: You will love the delicious dressing of these cupcakes so make sure to try this one!

Ingredients:

- Butter – 1 cup
- Caster sugar – 1 cup
- Vanilla extract – 2 tbsp.
- Eggs – 2
- Flour – 2 cups
- Baking powder – 2 tbsp.
- Cocoa powder – 2 tbsp.
- Buttermilk – 2 cups
- White vinegar – 1 tbsp.
- Bicarbonate soda – 1 tbsp.
- Red food color – 2 drops

Icing:

- Cream cheese – 2 cups
- Butter – 1 cup
- Icing sugar – 1 tbsp.
- Red food color – 2 drops

Directions:

1. Add butter into the bowl.
2. Mix caster sugar, vanilla extract, eggs, flour, baking powder, cocoa powder, buttermilk, white vinegar, soda and red food color.
3. Heat the oven to 350 F and prepare the muffin tins.
4. Insert paper cases in the tray and pour the batter into the paper cases.

5. Bake for 15 minutes.
6. Meanwhile, prepare the Icing: mix cream cheese, butter, icing sugar and red food coloring.
7. When ready, spread icing on each cupcake to serve!

Chapter 4: Easy To Make Cupcakes

Recipe 20: Coconut With Dark Chocolate Cupcakes

Cooking time: 15 minutes

Servings: 2

Description: The combination of dark chocolate and coconut makes this cupcake recipe so delicious that you wouldn't be able to get enough of it!

Ingredients:

- Cream cheese – 2 cups
- Butter – 2 cups
- Caster sugar – 1 tbsp.
- Eggs – 2
- Flour – 1 cup
- Cocoa powder – 1 tbsp.
- Milk – 2 cups

- Dark chocolate chips – 1 cup
- Coconut (shredded) – 1 cup
- Pink frosting – 1 cup

Directions:
1. Add butter into the bowl.
2. Mix cream cheese, caster sugar, eggs, flour, cocoa powder, milk and dark chocolate chips.
3. Heat the oven to 350 F and prepare the muffin tins.
4. Insert paper cases. Pour the batter into the paper cases.
5. Bake for 15 minutes.
6. When ready, spread pink frosting with sprinkling coconut to serve!

Recipe 21: Licorice Cupcakes

Cooking time: 15 minutes

Servings: 2

Description: Try the amazing licorice cupcake recipe and you will fall in love with it!

Ingredients:

- Licorice Teabags – 4
- Butter – 2 cups
- Caster sugar – 1 cup
  Eggs – 2
- Pistachios – 1 cup
- Flour – 2 cups
- Almond milk – 1 cup
- Licorice (sliced) to decorate

Icing:

- Pistachios – 1 cup
- Caster sugar – 1 cup
- Salt flakes – 1 tbsp.
- Vanilla essence – 1 tbsp.
- Water – 1 cup
- Green food color – 2 drops
- Cream – 2 tbsp.

Directions:
1. Add licorice teabags into the bowl.
2. Mix butter, caster sugar, eggs, pistachios, flour and almond milk.
3. Heat the oven to 350 F and prepare the muffin tins.
4. Insert paper cases into the tins and pour the batter into the paper cases.
5. Bake for 15 minutes.
6. Meanwhile, prepare the **Icing:** mix pistachios, caster sugar, salt flakes, vanilla essence, water, green food color and cream into the bowl.
7. When cupcakes are ready, spread the icing with licorice slice on each to serve!

Recipe 22: White Chocolate Cupcakes

Cooking time: 15 minutes

Servings: 2

Description: My children loves this white chocolate recipe so much that I always have to have it on our family treat tray!

Ingredients:

- Butter – 2 cups
- White chocolate – 2 cups

- Caster sugar – 1 cup
- Egg – 1
- Flour – 2 cups
- Vanilla bean – 1 tbsp.
- Silver cachous to sprinkle

Icing:

- White chocolate – 2 cups
- Cream – 2 cups
- Pink food color – 2 drops

Directions:
1. Add butter into the bowl.
2. Mix white chocolate, caster sugar, egg, flour and vanilla bean.
3. Heat the oven to 350 F and prepare the muffin tins.
4. Insert paper cases into the tins and pour the batter into the paper cases.
5. Bake for 15 minutes.
6. Meanwhile, prepare the **Icing:** mix white chocolate, cream and pink food color.
7. When ready, spread the icing with sprinkling silver cachous to serve!

Recipe 23: Mango Puree Cupcakes

Cooking time: 15 minutes

Servings: 2

Description: Try this delicious recipe of mango puree cupcake and you will surely love it!

Ingredients:

- Cupcake powder recipe – 1 pack

- Coconut shredded – 2 cups
- Mango puree – 1 cup
- Icing sugar – 1 cup
- Warm milk – 2 cups

Directions:
1. Add cupcake powder into the bowl.
2. Mix coconut, mango puree, icing sugar and milk.
3. Heat the oven to 350 F and prepare the muffin tins.
4. Insert paper cases. Pour the batter into the paper cases.
5. Bake for 15 minutes.
6. When ready, serve and enjoy!

Recipe 24: Raspberries White Choco Cupcakes

Cooking time: 15 minutes

Servings: 2

Description: You will love the flavor of this recipe so make sure to try it at home tonight!

Ingredients:

- Butter – 2 cups
- Caster sugar – 2 cups
- Eggs – 2
- White chocolate – 2 cups
- Flour – 2 cups
- Milk – 2 cups
- Raspberries – 1 cup

Icing:

- White chocolate – 1 cup
- Cream – 2 cups

- Butter – 1 cup

Directions:
1. Add butter into the bowl.
2. Mix caster sugar, eggs, white chocolate, flour, milk and raspberries.
3. Heat the oven to 350 F and prepare the muffin tins.
4. Insert paper cases. Pour the batter into the paper cases.
5. Bake for 15 minutes.
6. Meanwhile prepare the **Icing:** mix white chocolate, cream and butter.
7. When ready, spread the icing on cupcakes to serve!

Recipe 25: Red Cupcakes

Cooking time: 15 minutes

Servings: 2

Description: You might need to gather a few more ingredients more than other recipes but I can assure you that it is going to be worth it!

Ingredients:

- Flour – 2 cups
- Cocoa powder -1 tbsp.
- Bicarbonate soda – 1 tsp.
- Baking powder – 2 tbsp.
- Caster sugar – ½ cup
- Buttermilk – 2 cups
- Eggs – 2
- Vegetable oil – 2 tbsp.
- Red food color – 2 tbsp.
- White vinegar – 2 tbsp.

- Cream cheese – ½ packet
- Icing sugar – ½ cup
- Vanilla extract – 2 tbsp.

Directions:
1. Add flour into the bowl.
2. Mix cocoa powder, soda, baking powder, caster sugar, buttermilk, eggs, oil and white vinegar.
3. Heat the oven to 350 F and prepare the muffin tins.
4. Insert paper cases. Pour the batter into the paper cases.
5. Bake for 15 minutes.
6. Meanwhile prepare the icing with mixing cream cheese, icing sugar and vanilla extract.
7. When cupcakes are ready, spread the icing on top to serve!

Cupcakes Recipes

Chocolate Cupcakes With Caramel Frosting

(Prep time20 min, cook 20min, ready in 1hr 40min.)

Makes 15 cupcakes

Ingredients:

- 1 cup white sugar
- 2 cups all-purpose flour
- ¼ cup unsweetened cocoa powder
- 2 teaspoons baking soda
- 1 cup water
- 2 tablespoons grape jelly
- 1 cup mayonnaise
- 1 teaspoon vanilla extract
- ¼ cup melted butter
- 1/3 cup half-and-half cream

- ¾ cup packed brown sugar
- ½ teaspoon vanilla extract
- ¾ cups confectioners' sugar

Preparation:

1. Preheat oven to 350 degrees F (175 degrees C). Grease 15 muffin cups or line with paper baking cups.
2. In a large bowl, stir together the white sugar, flour, cocoa, and baking soda. Make a well in the center, and pour in the water, grape jelly, mayonnaise, and 1 teaspoon of vanilla. Mix just until blended. Spoon the batter into the prepared cups, dividing evenly.
3. Bake in the preheated oven until the tops spring back when lightly pressed, 20 to 25 minutes. Cool in the pan set over a wire rack. When cool, arrange the cupcakes on a serving platter.
4. Make the frosting while the cupcakes cool. Combine the butter, half-and-half and brown sugar in a medium saucepan. Bring to a boil, stirring frequently. Remove from the heat and stir in the confectioners' sugar and vanilla. Set the pan over a bowl of ice water and whisk or beat with an electric mixer until fluffy. Frost cupcakes when they are completely cool.

Chocolate Beer Cupcakes With Whiskey Filling And Irish Cream Icing

(Prep time 30min, cook 20min, ready in 1hr 25min.)

Makes 24 cupcakes

Ingredients:

- 1 cup Irish stout beer (such as Guinness)
- 1 cup butter
- ¾ cup unsweetened cocoa powder
- 2 cups all-purpose flour
- 2 cups white sugar
- ½ teaspoon baking soda
- ¾ teaspoon salt
- 2 large eggs
- 2/3 cup sour cream
- 2/3 heavy whipping cream
- 8 ounces bittersweet chocolate, chopped
- 2 tablespoons butter
- 1 teaspoon Irish whiskey or more according to your taste.

Preparation:

1. Preheat oven to 350 degrees F (175 degrees C).
2. Line 24 muffin cups with paper liners.
3. Bring Irish stout beer and 1 cup butter to a boil in a saucepan and set aside until butter has melted, stirring occasionally. Mix in cocoa powder until smooth.
4. Whisk together flour, sugar, baking soda, and salt in a bowl until thoroughly combined.
5. Beat eggs with sour cream in a large bowl with an electric mixer on low until well combined. Slowly beat in the beer mixture, then the flour mixture; beat until the batter is smooth.
6. Divide batter between the prepared cupcake cups, filling each cup about 2/3 full.
7. Bake in the preheated oven until a toothpick inserted into the center of a cupcake comes out clean, about 17 minutes.
8. Cool the cupcakes completely. Cut cores out of the center of each cupcake with a sharp paring knife. Discard cores.
9. Bring cream to a simmer in a saucepan over low heat; stir in bittersweet chocolate until melted.
10. Mix in 2 tablespoons butter and Irish whiskey until butter is melted; let mixture cool to room temperature. Filling will thicken as it cools.
11. Spoon the filling into the cored cupcakes.
12. For frosting, whip 1/2 cup butter in a bowl with an electric mixer until fluffy, 2 to 3 minutes.
13. Set mixer to low speed and slowly beat in confectioners' sugar, 1 cup at a time, until frosting is smooth and spreadable. Beat in the Irish cream liqueur; adjust thickness of frosting with more confectioners' sugar if needed.
14. Spread frosting on filled cupcakes.

Dark Chocolate Bacon Cupcakes

(Prep time 15min, cook 25min, ready in 40min.)

Makes 24 cupcakes.

Ingredients:

- 12 slices bacon
- 2 cups all-purpose flour
- ¾ unsweetened cocoa powder
- 2 cups white sugar
- 2 teaspoons baking soda
- 1 teaspoon baking powder
- ½ teaspoon sea salt
- 2 eggs
- 1 cup strong brewed coffee
- 1 cup buttermilk
- ½ cup vegetable oil
- 1 tablespoon unsweetened cocoa powder for dusting

Preparation:

1. Preheat oven to 375 degrees F (190 degrees C). Place bacon in a large, deep skillet. Cook over medium-high heat until evenly brown. Drain, crumble and set aside.
2. In a large bowl, stir together the flour, 3/4 cup cocoa powder, sugar, baking soda, baking powder and salt. Make a well in the center and pour in the eggs, coffee, buttermilk and oil. Stir just until blended. Mix in 3/4 of the bacon, reserving the rest for garnish. Spoon the batter into the prepared cups, dividing evenly.
3. Bake in the preheated oven until the tops spring back when lightly pressed, 20 to 25 minutes. Cool in the pan set over a wire rack. When cool, arrange the cupcakes on a serving platter. Frost with your favorite chocolate frosting and sprinkle reserved bacon crumbles on top. Dust with additional cocoa powder.

Chili Chocolate Cupcakes With Chili Cream Cheese Frosting

(Prep time 20min, cook 18min ready in 1hr 18min.)

Makes 24 cupcakes

Ingredients:

- One 18.25 ounce chocolate cake mix
- 1½ teaspoons ground ancho chili pepper
- ¼ teaspoons cayenne pepper
- 1¼ cups water
- 1/3 vegetable oil
- 3 eggs
- 1 teaspoon ground ancho chili pepper
- 1/8 teaspoon cayenne pepper
- ½ teaspoon ground cinnamon
- 4 cups white sugar
- One 8 ounce package softened cream cheese
- ½ cup softened butter
- ½ teaspoon vanilla extract
- 24 small dried red chilies.

Preparation:

1. Preheat oven to 350 degrees F (175 degrees C). Line 24 cupcake cups with paper liners.

2. Empty the boxed cake mix into a mixing bowl, and whisk in 1 1/2 teaspoon of ground ancho chili and 1/4 teaspoon of cayenne pepper. Using an electric mixer on medium speed, beat in the water, vegetable oil, and eggs; beat for 2 minutes. Spoon the batter into the prepared cupcake cups, filling them 2/3 full.

3. Bake in the preheated oven until a toothpick inserted into the center of a cupcake comes out clean, 18 to 22 minutes. Remove and cool completely before frosting.

4. In a bowl, sift 1 teaspoon of ground ancho chili, 1/8 teaspoon of cayenne pepper, and the cinnamon with the confectioners' sugar. Beat in the cream cheese and butter with an electric mixer on medium speed until the frosting is smooth; mix in the vanilla extract. Spread the frosting onto the cooled cupcakes in attractive swirls, and poke a small dried chili, stem-side up, into the frosting as a garnish.

Cherry Coke Cupcakes

(Prep time 20min, cook 20min, ready in 1hr 10min.)

Makes 12 cupcakes

Ingredients:

- One 15.25 ounce chocolate cake mix
- 1 can cherry flavored cola
- 2 cups heavy whipping cream
- ¼ cup confectioners' sugar
- One 12.5 ounce can cherry pie filling

- **12 cherries.**

Preparation:

1. Preheat oven to 350 degrees F (175 degrees C). Line 12 muffin cups with paper liners.
2. Mix cake mix and cherry-flavored cola together in a bowl until batter is smooth. Spoon batter into prepared muffin cups about 2/3 full.
3. Bake in the preheated oven until muffins spring back when lightly touched, 18 to 23 minutes. Cool in the pan for 10 minutes before removing to cool completely on a wire rack.
4. Beat cream in a large bowl using an electric mixer until frothy; beat in confectioners' sugar until stiff peaks form. Lift your beater or whisk straight up: the frosting will form sharp peaks; refrigerate.
5. Cut a well out of the top center of each cupcake and fill with 2 to 3 cherries from the cherry pie filling. Transfer frosting to a piping bag or a plastic bag with 1 corner cut off. Frost cupcakes and top each with a maraschino cherry.

German Chocolate Cupcakes

(Prep time 25min, cook 25min ready 1hr 20 min.)

Makes 12 cupcakes

Ingredients:

Chocolate-Pecan ice cream frosting:
- ½ gallon chocolate ice cream
- ¾ cup toasted pecan pieces

Cupcakes:
- 1 cup all-purpose flour
- ½ teaspoon baking soda
- ¼ teaspoon salt
- Two 1 ounce squares sweet baking chocolate
- ¼ cup water
- ½ cup softened butter
- ½ cup sugar
- 2 eggs
- ½ teaspoon vanilla
- ½ cup buttermilk or sour milk
- Caramel ice cream topping
- 2/3 toasted shaved coconut

Preparation:

1. Chocolate-Pecan Ice Cream: Line a cookie sheet with waxed paper; set aside. Slice chocolate ice cream into sheets about 2 inches thick. Use a cookie cutter to cut rounds just larger than the cupcakes from frozen ice cream. Place on waxed paper-lined cookie sheet. Press toasted pecan pieces into ice cream letting pecans protrude from the ice cream. Cover and freeze 4 hours or overnight.

2. Preheat oven to 350 degrees F. Line twelve 2-1/2-inch muffin cups with paper baking cups. Set aside.
3. In a small bowl stir together flour, baking soda, and salt; set aside.
4. In a small saucepan combine chocolate and water. Cook and stir over low heat until melted; cool about 10 minutes.
5. In a large bowl beat butter with an electric mixer on medium to high speed for 30 seconds. Beat in sugar until fluffy. Add eggs and vanilla; beat on low speed until combined then beat on medium speed for 1 minute. Beat in chocolate mixture. Add the flour mixture and buttermilk alternately to beaten mixture, beating on low speed after each addition just until combined. Spoon batter into bake cups, filling cups about 2/3 full.
6. Bake about 25 minutes or until a wooden toothpick comes out clean. Cool in pans on wire racks for 10 minutes. Remove from pans. Cool thoroughly.
7. Just before serving, heat caramel ice cream topping until warm. Remove wrappers from cupcakes; place cupcakes on plates or in shallow bowls. Top each cupcake with one round of Chocolate-Pecan Ice Cream "Frosting." Top with toasted coconut and drizzle with warm caramel ice cream topping.

Chocolate Chip Cheesecake Cupcakes

(Prep time 20min, cook 25min, ready in 1hr 15min.)

Makes 24 cupcakes

Ingredients:

- One 18.25 ounce chocolate cake mix
- 1¼ cups water
- 4 divided eggs
- ½ cup vegetable oil
- One 8 ounce package cream cheese
- 2/3 cups white sugar
- ¾ teaspoon vanilla extract
- ¾ cup miniature chocolate chips
- One 16 ounce container cream cheese frosting

Preparation:

1. Preheat oven to 350 degrees F (175 degrees C). Line 24 muffin cups with paper liners.
2. Combine cake mix, water, 3 eggs, and oil together in a bowl using an electric mixer until batter is smooth, about 2 minutes. Spoon batter into the prepared muffin cups.
3. Blend cream cheese, sugar, 1 egg, and vanilla extract together in a blender until cheesecake filling is smooth; stir in 1/2 cup chocolate chips. Spoon about 1 tablespoon cheesecake filling into each cupcake.
4. Bake in the preheated oven until a toothpick inserted into a cupcake comes out clean, about 25 minutes. Cool cupcakes on a wire rack.
5. Frost each cupcake with cream cheese frosting and sprinkle remaining chocolate chips over each cupcake.

Chocolate-Orange Cupcakes With Pistachio Buttercream

(Prep time 20min, cook 20 min, ready in 1hr 10min.)

Makes 12 cupcakes

Ingredients:

- 1½ all-purpose flour
- 1 cup white sugar
- 3 tablespoons cocoa powder
- 1 teaspoon baking soda
- ¼ teaspoon salt
- 1 cup cold water
- 1/3 cup olive oil
- 2 tablespoons orange juice
- ½ teaspoon vanilla extract
- 1 tablespoon grated orange zest

Icing:

- ½ cup butter
- 2/3 cup confectioners' sugar
- 2 tablespoons instant pistachio pudding mix
- 2 tablespoons cold water
- 1 ounce dark chocolate

Preparation:

1. Preheat oven to 350 degrees F (175 degrees C). Grease 12 muffin cups with shortening using a paper towel and dust with about 1 teaspoon flour or line with paper liners.
2. Combine 1 1/2 cups flour, white sugar, cocoa powder, baking soda, and salt in the bowl of a stand mixer. Beat 1 cup cold water, olive oil, orange juice, and vanilla extract into flour mixture on medium-low speed until batter is just combined, about 2 minutes. Fold orange zest into batter. Pour batter into prepared muffin cups, 2/3-full.
3. Bake in the preheated oven until a toothpick inserted into a cupcake comes out clean, about 20 minutes. Transfer cupcakes to a wire rack to cool completely, about 30 minutes.
4. Beat butter in a bowl using an electric mixer in medium speed until fluffy, about 1 minute. Slowly pour confectioners' sugar into creamed butter and beat until incorporated, about 2 minutes. Beat pudding mix into butter mixture until just combined. Add water, 1 tablespoon at a time, until desired consistency of icing is reached. Ice the cooled cupcakes; garnish with grated chocolate.

Lemon Cupcakes

(Prep time 50min, cook17 min, ready in 1hr 25min.)

Makes 30 cupcakes

Ingredients:

- 3 cups self-rising flour
- ½ teaspoon salt
- 1 cup butter
- 2 cups white sugar
- 4 eggs
- 1 teaspoon vanilla extract
- 2 tablespoons lemon zest
- 1 cup whole milk
- 2½ tablespoons fresh lemon juice

Lemon Cream icing:

- 2 cups chilled heavy cream
- ¾ cup confectioners' sugar
- 1½ tablespoon fresh lemon juice

Preparation:

1. Preheat oven to 375 degrees F (190 degrees C). Line 30 cupcake pan cups with paper liners.
2. Sift the self-rising flour and salt together in a bowl. In another bowl, beat the unsalted butter and sugar with an electric mixer until light and fluffy. Beat in the eggs one at a time, beating each egg until incorporated before adding the next. Mix in the vanilla extract and lemon zest.
3. Gently beat the flour mixture into the butter mixture, one third at a time, alternating with half the milk and half the lemon juice after each of the first 2 additions of flour. Beat until just combined; do not over mix.
4. Fill the prepared cupcake liners with batter 3/4 full, and bake in the preheated oven until a toothpick inserted in the center comes out clean, about 17 minutes. Let the cupcakes cool in the pans for about 10 minutes before removing them to finish cooling on a rack.
5. To make the icing, beat the cream in a chilled bowl with an electric mixer set on Low until the cream begins to thicken. Add the confectioners' sugar and lemon juice, a little at a time, beating after each addition, until fully incorporated. Increase the mixer speed to High, and beat until the icing forms soft peaks, about 5 minutes. Spread on the cooled cupcakes.

Lemon Frosted Carrot Cake Cupcakes

(Prep time 30min, cook 18min, ready in 55min.)

Makes 24 cupcakes

Ingredients:

- 2 cups all-purpose flour
- 1 cup granulated sugar
- 2 teaspoons ground cinnamon
- 1 teaspoon baking powder
- 1 teaspoon baking soda
- ¼ teaspoon ground nutmeg
- 1/8 teaspoon salt
- 2 cups shredded carrots
- ½ cup canola oil
- ½ cup unsweetened applesauce
- 1 lightly beaten egg
- 1 teaspoon vanilla
- 1 cup flaked toasted coconut
- 1 cup jelly beans or chocolate egg candies

Lemon cream cheese frosting:

- 3 ounces softened cream cheese
- 3 tablespoons butter
- 2 tablespoons lemon curd
- 3 cups powdered sugar
- 2 teaspoons milk

Preparation:

1. Preheat oven to 350 degrees F. Line muffin pans with 24 Baking Cups.
2. Combine flour, sugar, cinnamon, baking powder, baking soda, nutmeg, and salt in a large bowl.

3. Combine the carrots, oil, applesauce, egg, and vanilla in a medium bowl. Add carrot mixture to the flour mixture; mix just until combined. Divide the batter among the prepared muffin cups.

4. Bake 16 to 18 minutes or until a toothpick inserted in centers comes out clean. Cool 5 minutes in muffin pan. Transfer cupcakes to cooling rack; cool completely.

5. Top with Lemon Cream Cheese Frosting, reserving a small amount. Make "nests" with the coconut. Dip jelly beans or candy eggs slightly into extra frosting and then place in the "nests" to keep them in place.

6. Lemon Cream Cheese Frosting: Combine cream cheese, butter, softened; and lemon curd in a large mixing bowl. Beat with an electric mixer on medium to high speed until smooth. Gradually add 1 1/2 cups of powdered sugar, beating well. Beat in 2 teaspoons milk. Gradually beat in another 1 1/2 cups powdered sugar. If necessary, beat in additional milk, 1 teaspoon at a time, to reach spreading consistency.

Real Strawberry Cupcakes

(Prep time 40min, cook 20min, ready in 1hr 15min.)

Makes 12 cupcakes

Ingredients:

- 8 large fresh strawberries
- 2 eggs
- 1 cup white sugar
- 1/3 cup vegetable oil
- ½ teaspoon vanilla extract
- ½ teaspoon lemon zest
- 1½ cups all-purpose flour
- 2 teaspoons baking powder
- ¼ teaspoon salt
- ¾ cup softened cream cheese
- 2 tablespoons butter
- ½ confectioners' sugar
- ½ tablespoon vanilla extract
- 3 sliced large fresh strawberries

Preparation:

1. Preheat oven to 325 degrees F (165 degrees C). Spray cupcake cups with cooking spray, or line with cupcake liners.
2. Place 8 strawberries into a blender, and blend until smooth. Pour the puree through a strainer to remove seeds. Puree should equal about 3/4 cup. Set the puree aside.
3. In a large bowl, beat together the eggs, white sugar, vegetable oil, 1/2 teaspoon vanilla extract, lemon zest, and strawberry puree until well combined. Stir in the flour, baking powder, salt, vanilla pudding mix (for a moister cupcake), and red food coloring to reach a desired shade of pink. Spoon the batter into the prepared cupcake cups, filling each about 2/3 full.
4. Bake in the preheated oven until the cupcakes have risen and a toothpick inserted into the center of a cupcake comes

out clean, about 23 minutes. Allow the cupcakes to cool at least 10 minutes before frosting.

5. To make frosting, beat cream cheese and butter together in a mixing bowl with an electric mixer until smooth, and mix in confectioners' sugar and 1/2 teaspoon vanilla extract to make a lump-free icing. Frost each cupcake with about 2 tablespoons of icing, and top each cupcake with a strawberry slice.

Sin-Fully Delicious Chocolate Cupcakes

(Prep time 20min, cook 15min ready in 1hr 5min.)

Makes 24 cupcakes

Ingredients:

- One 18.25 ounce chocolate cake mix
- 1 cup milk
- 3 eggs
- ½ cup melted butter
- 1 teaspoon ground cinnamon

- 1 teaspoon vanilla extract

Icing:
- ½ cup butter
- ½ cup butter-flavoured shortening
- 1 pinch sea salt
- 1 teaspoon vanilla extract
- 1 tablespoon cinnamon
- 1 tablespoon unsweetened cocoa powder
- 3 cups confectioners' sugar
- ¼ cup milk

Preparation:

1. Preheat an oven to 350 degrees F (175 degrees C).
2. Line 24 muffin cups with paper liners.
3. Beat together the chocolate cake mix, 1 cup milk, eggs, 1/2 cup melted butter, 1 teaspoon cinnamon, and 1 teaspoon vanilla extract in a bowl with an electric mixer on low speed until moist. Beat for 2 more minutes on medium speed.
4. Fill each muffin cup about 2/3 full of batter.
5. Sprinkle the cupcakes with cinnamon sugar.
6. Bake in the preheated oven until a toothpick inserted into the center comes out clean, about 15 minutes.
7. Cool in the pans for 10 minutes before removing to cool completely on a wire rack.
8. Cream together 1/2 cup butter and shortening in a bowl until smooth.
9. Stir in sea salt, 1 teaspoon vanilla extract, 1 tablespoon cinnamon, cocoa powder, and 3 cups confectioners' sugar.
10. Stir in milk.
11. Mix in 2 more cups confectioners' sugar or as needed until desired consistency is achieved.
12. Spread the frosting on the cooled cupcakes.

Frosted Peppermint Mini Bites

(Prep time 15min, cook 15min, ready in 1hr 10min.)

Makes 66 mini bites

Ingredients:

- ¾ cup Ghirardelli premium baking coca
- 1½ cups all-purpose flour
- 1½ cups sugar
- 1½ teaspoons baking soda
- ¾ teaspoons salt
- 2 large eggs
- ¾ cup warm water
- ¾ cup buttermilk
- 3 tablespoons sunflower oil
- 1 teaspoon pure peppermint extract
- Peppermint candies coarsely chopped for garnish.

Frosting:

- 3 sticks unsalted butter
- 1 pound confectioners' sugar
- 1 teaspoon pure vanilla extract

Preparation:

1. For Bites: Line mini-muffin tins with mini-paper liners. Mix all ingredients (except crushed peppermint candies) to create a chocolate batter. Divide batter among muffin cups, filling each 2/3 full. Bake until a toothpick inserted into centers comes out clean, about 10 minutes. Let cool in tins on wire racks.
2. For Frosting: Beat butter with a mixer on medium-high speed until pale and creamy, about 2 minutes. Reduce speed to medium. Add sugar, cup at a time, beating after each addition, about 5 minutes. Add vanilla, and beat until buttercream is smooth.
3. Frost each mini bite with buttercream frosting and garnish with peppermint candy.

Conclusion

If you love cupcakes, but you don't really have any experience in making them then this book is a great start with. With different flavors, it is easy to make them for any occasion of the year. I always find, that a lot of people appreciate it when you home cook a little something for them as a gift, and with these recipes it won't require any extra effort which is why this is the perfect home cooked dessert to make.
I hope you have learned how easy it is to make cupcakes and that it is not a hassle like you think it is after all.

www.ingramcontent.com/pod-product-compliance
Lightning Source LLC
Chambersburg PA
CBHW070925080526
44589CB00013B/1428